Save Time & Money

3 Steps in the Mindset Inventory Exercise™

Step 1

Initial brainstorming activity

Step 2

The "frequent offenders" that you battle

Step 3

Why the limiting beliefs, negative self-talk…symptoms of something bigger…happen

Bonus (added content, only in the paperback version)

Power of Focus

I frequently use a phrase when I am speaking about or teaching on the topic of mindset: "Wherever you go, your mind is always there." That goes without saying, right!?! However, I believe it is worth stating because often times we are just on auto-pilot in most things that we do throughout the day and in any given situation.

When is the last time that you took time to think about what was going on in your mind, aside from some of the obvious moments? I know there are plenty of times that I am just going about my business, not paying much attention to what my mind is thinking, what it is processing or how it is impacting my very actions at that moment.

As I dive deeper into this subject, I want you to start paying attention to what is going on in your mind. Be more cognizant of your thoughts and the internal dialogue that naturally takes place. Ask yourself, "Am I in control of my mind?" I believe that is a valid question. Another valid, and likely more important question is, "Am I in control of my thoughts?" That gets a bit deeper into the core of things. The next logical question, at least to me, is, "Am I in control of my actions, behaviors and responses?"

If you are anything like me, you are becoming a bit more aware of what is going on inside your head right now. That's great, because that is exactly what I wanted to achieve. Now we are able to get down to business. You are more aware, more focused on what is happening between your ears, and, as a result of that, the ensuing actions, behaviors and responses.

Are you ready to learn the three steps that are going to create an immediate savings of time and money, and give you actions that you can take anywhere and at any time you need? I know you are, so let's get things going. But, before I do, I want to re-visit a question from the cover of the book. How much is it worth to you to NOT sit in someone's office to conduct a deep-dive into your mindset?

I conducted a little research, and the average cost, nationally, per hour for a counselor is $90, with the maximum being around $250 per hour. Consider reading this book to be about an average of an $80-$85 monetary savings, as well as at least 30 minutes saved, along with whatever travel time you would add to that, if not conducting it virtually.

So, you can see that there is benefit and value in what you have invested in for yourself. I asked that question here to not only help you keep in mind that you can conduct this deep-dive exercise anytime and anywhere you need to, but also to show that you have made a wise minimal investment.

You get to decide how and when you use it. You will be able to use the three-step exercise no matter the situation, especially when there are known challenges, new opportunities and various limiting factors that are present. In other words, you can be the master of your mind, and create changes to allow you to reap the benefits immediately, as well as in the future.

Once you recognize what is happening, you can then take action, but you have to first identify so you can take action. You can't effectively act on something that is unknown. That is why the very first step in this exercise is geared toward the identification process. Before we get started on this exercise, I do want to provide a bit of advice. It has been my experience, both personally and professionally, that the best way to get the most out of this exercise is to:

1) Put away all distractions (phone, computer/email, any other device that could distract you and anyone else that might be doing this alongside you.

2) You want to truly commit to this process, so commit to being 100% engaged. If not, perhaps this is not the exercise/mini-course for you.

If the latter is the case and you aren't committed, I will work with you for a full refund. I would not want you to waste your money, nor would I want to have a committed group unknowingly impacted.

Disclaimer: As you work on this Mindset Inventory Exercise, you might become emotionally challenged as you go deeper into your mind to discover not only the common thoughts that are present in your mind. Higher Calling Consulting, LLC, and its principal, Rich Parsons, are not responsible for emotional distress as a result of a deep-dive into the mindset. Rich Parsons can assist in the exploration process of your mindset, but not beyond the basic coaching. Rest assured that anything shared is not going anywhere, with the exception of expected or expressed harm to self or others.

Before you get any further into this, I want to share a few administrative notes with you, that will allow you to make the most out of your time. Ideally, you are in a quiet place where you can think clearly, without distraction (especially any electronic devices or know environment factors), for the duration of the time spent completing the three steps. All you need to complete this exercise is a couple pieces of paper and a pen or pencil. That's it…pretty simple, huh?!?

Now let's look at the first step in this exercise.

<u>Step 1</u>

The first step is the most important in the process, because it sets the stage for the next two steps. Without properly completing this step, the rest will be impacted. So, the more committed you are to the process, the better your results will be. You will need to take the blinders off, so to speak, and open your mind to fully explore the thoughts and feelings that are present. When you take the time to dig deep and recall thought and feelings, you are able to make the most progress.

I want you to think of a couple situations where you were taking on something new, challenging or out of your comfort zone. Perhaps you bring to mind a new duty position or role, a new job, a task that is vastly different from anything you've done before, a goal that is a stretch for you, a speech, a paper that is due on an unexpected topic, etc. I think you get the point, think of situations that might typically be a bit of a stressor for you.

Perhaps what you are doing right now is one of those things. Anything that is new, out of the norm, challenging or a stretch, will do the trick. If you are anything like me, you likely have several ideas in mind.

Now, with situations and scenarios in mind, I'll ask you to take the allotted time (go-time given below), or really whatever amount of time you need…this is your exercise, I am just the facilitator for you…to jot down as many of the negative ideas, thoughts, limiting beliefs, negative self-talk, fear, doubt…anything that has a likelihood of holding you back from doing something freely.

As you complete this step or the exercise, I encourage you to also be mindful of the one or two-offs that might pop into your mind as well. By that I mean, if you have mostly "negative" thoughts, but there one or two that are more "positive" in nature, then I want you to jot them down on the side. Same if you are primarily a pretty positive-minded person, if there are any opposites that come to mind, write them down on the side as well. There is a method to my madness with those one or two-off thoughts.

Okay…pull out a pen/pencil and piece of paper, then take the next 5 minutes or so to complete this first step in the Mindset Inventory Exercise™, then we will be ready to review and move on to the next topic. Come right back when you are ready. Again, you are writing down as many things that you can think of, and you are really in control of the time used.

Now that you are complete with the first step, I want you to take just a moment to look at what you have written down on the paper. I will ask you a couple questions before moving on to Step Two.

- Do you feel you were open and honest with yourself?

- Did you discover anything that had not really dawned on you that much before now?

- Did you take enough time to complete the first step as fully as you wanted? If not, feel free to continue…this is your time!

- What did you learn based on your thoughts and responses to the question?

If we were in a live/in-person session, I would ask you those questions, and perhaps have a couple people share if they felt so compelled.

As we move into the second step, I will again encourage you to be all-in on this exercise. Without that mindset, you will not gain the most out each step and the process as a whole. There are learning opportunities no matter where you look, as long as you are looking at and for the right stuff.

Step 2

With your initial list complete, some time to reflect and a few questions answered, you are now ready for the second step. Fortunately, the initial hard work has been completed. Your next step is pretty simple to complete, but it does take a little more thought to make it happen.

Out of all that you have written down, I want you to look at the words and phrases, and circle the most common examples of the thoughts, beliefs and feelings that you recall being present in just about every event, scenario or situation. This, again, can be a bit challenging, but I know you can do it, because you have already completed one of the most important parts.

Here you go…another 3-5 minutes to circle the "frequent offenders" on your list.

GO!

When complete, you can take a break or whatever you need, because Step 3 is going to be where we/you really get down to business.

-----Take a Break if Needed-----

If you stepped away from your book, welcome back! You have completed some pretty amazing work so far. You completed a portion of an exercise that not a lot of people would be comfortable completing. If you are like most people who've completed the exercise, you are a bit shocked at what you have before you.

When was the last time you really took time to make a deliberate look at yourself, your mind and put something down on paper? While you might've had some or all of this already identified in your head, there is something special about writing things down.

I was watching a video and reading up on a topic the other day, where the presenter spoke about the staggering amount of information that is forgotten within set periods of time.

Kohn, shared that research on the forgetting curve shows that within one hour, people will lose an average of 50 percent of the information presented to them. Within 24

hours, they have forgotten, on average, 70 percent of new information, and within a week, about 90 percent is forgotten. That is amazing!

You know what helps stem the loss of information, writing things down, just as you have done here. When we identify something and create notes, we are more likely to recall it later on. Mark Murphy shares in an online Forbes Magazine article, that when we generate something, we are reducing the likelihood of losing the information, slowly, then possibly forever.

However, according the neuroscientists, when we generate/create something ourselves (i.e., write it out, or even type, but best to write), we are more likely to retain that information for a longer period than if they would've simply read it and not written anything down (Murphy, 2018).

Okay, so I have given you some support to digest, so it is not just my thoughts and beliefs that are being presented here. There is value in exploring and writing things down, just as you have done thus far.

The next portion of the exercise is likely going to be the

most challenging part for you, as it is for most people. I say that because, it really requires a person (you) to get down and dirty with yourself. You can't just scratch the surface here and get the results you are looking for. If you wanted an absolute quick fix, then, well, you are not in the right place or reading the right content. However, I assure you, if you allow yourself to go where this needs to go, you can make some serious headway in getting the results you are really after.

You can absolutely set yourself up for the follow-on lessons in the series/course that this is pulled from. In Mastering Your Mind™, students learn three Mastery Tips, some easy-to-complete and powerful Action Steps, as well as learn about the Power of Focus to wrap it up. More on that later on.

For now, though, if you are ready to get down to business and take steps for what could potentially be the breakthrough moment for you, then let's go. If completed properly, this can be the icing on the cake and a gamechanger for your mindset, which will impact other aspects of your life.

<u>Step 3</u>

In this third and final step, you will take the results of the first two steps, specially step two, and start to dig into things more in-depth to find the root cause and any triggers.

I will, again, make the disclaimer that this could be challenging for some people, more than others, so please use good personal judgement when delving into the deeper aspects of why certain limiting beliefs, negative self-talk, fear, doubt, etc., are so deeply rooted.

With the "frequent offenders" identified, you know which ones are most likely to surface during any number of situations and scenarios. Since they are the most common, it makes sense to start looking at and exploring them on a deeper level.

The activity for this portion of the exercise is not timed. I do not want to place any limits on the amount of time you spend exploring your mind, your heart and your inner-most being.

You should take a new piece of paper, and write down the "frequent offenders" that you identified in step two of the exercise. I ask that you now reflect on the words and/or phrases that you have on your paper.

I will ask you a few questions to generate some thought.

- Is there one, if more than one exists, that is the most common and/or problematic for you? If so, circle it so you can focus more attention on it.

- Do you see any common threads that run between any of the words or phrases you have listed? If so, take a moment to jot down a few memory-jogger words.

- Is there anything about the words/phrases that piques your interest or perhaps creates a unique feeling for you?

- Is there anything from your present or past that you feel is a contributing factor for why these words/phrases are commonly present in your mind?

- If there is something from the present or past that is a contributing factor, have you already had opportunity to address this matter with anyone, or even with yourself?

- Is there anything that you are afraid of exploring or finding out if you dig further into your associated thoughts and feelings?

- Are you in a good place and willing to go further in exploring so you can find the root cause for the thoughts and feelings that are presented on the surface?

These are the results/symptoms of whatever lies under the surface or even deeper rooted. It can be like an iceberg…you see 10-20 percent, but the remainder lies beneath.

I believe you get the point of where this final step in the Mindset Inventory Exercise™ is going. I encourage you to keep exploring, if not yet complete or to a satisfactory place. If you need support, please reach out to someone in your support network.

I am happy to connect with you to discuss procedural details and answer questions related to the exercise and process as a whole.

Here are a few general questions…not related to the final step.

- How do you feel right now?

- What did you get out of that exercise?

- Where is the value, for you, in completing the process?

In the Mastering Your Mind™ course, I share that digging into a root cause and/or trigger is like getting a pesky weed out of your yard (obviously a simple analogy). If you do not dig down below the surface a little, to find the root, the weed can be plucked up or the top cut off all you want, but it will continue to come back until it is pulled from the root. Deep-rooted thoughts and feelings are much the same.

In this last step, digging deep enough is required to start a true transformation. In this exercise, you have completed the first step in a larger process, but this first step is by far the most important. You can't work on that which is either not identified or is a blind spot for you.

You have completed the first of part of what I call R3 or the 3Rs. The first R is Recognize. The next steps are to work on the other two Rs: Replace and Reshape.

You have accomplished so much and I am happy for you. I pray that you have the results that you were looking for…and more! You should, at a minimum, have a good idea of the fiery darts that come your way and attack your mind. I imagine you also discovered which of those fiery darts are lobbed at you more frequently than others. And, if you dug deep into things, you have a new understanding of the root causes, and possibly the triggers, for what takes place in your mind.

I envision you being better equipped and more powerful than you've ever been before, and ready to take on the battles that will come your way. While you can't always control what is thrown at you, or what thoughts and feelings creep into the mix, you can, however, be in control of what happens as a result. You Recognize, then work to Replace and Reshape your mind.

If you want to dig deeper and work on the other two Rs, I have the perfect solution for you, which is offered in a do-it-yourself course, that comes with an opportunity for follow-on individual or group coaching calls.

You can contact me to setup a complimentary Success Call to discuss options and see if there is a good fit for you. My goal is to make sure you are setup for success for any situation that you face. At a minimum, I'd love to connect to hear directly from you about your experience with this book and the Mindset Inventory Exercise™.

I'd love to get a testimonial from you as well. Feel free to send a video or typed out testimonial to me via email (on the last page).

<u>Click here</u> to connect with me to setup your personal Success Call and/or share your feedback, results and/or testimonial.

Remember, "No matter where you go, your mind is always there!"

Fight for the battleground that is in your mind. You are destined to win…make the victory yours. With a Renewed Mind, you are setup for Victory!

Quick Recap of the 3 Steps in the Mindset Inventory Exercise™

1) Use a piece of paper and pen/pencil. Write out your negative thoughts and feelings (limiting beliefs, negative self-talk, fear, doubt, etc.)

2) Of those identified in Step 1, circle the "frequent offenders" to identify those that are most commonly there...no matter the situation.

3) In this final step, you sought out the root causes/triggers for the symptoms/outcomes that are presenting themselves. Don't take this lightly, in that it can get deep and there can be some emotional events associated with it. Digging into the depth of one's self is challenging.

If completed appropriately, this is likely a game-changer for people. I encourage you to keep digging deeper, and allow the growth to happen. Only you can do this, but you can get help, if/when needed.

References:

Kohn, A. (2014). Brain Science - The Forgetting Curve. Learning Solutions…https://learningsolutionsmag.com/articles/1379/brain-science-the-forgetting-curvethe-dirty-secret-of-corporate-training

Murphy, M. (2018). Neuroscience Explains Why You Need to Write Down...https://www.forbes.com/sites/markmurphy/2018/04/15/neuroscience-explains-why-you-need-to-write-down-your-goals-if-you-actually-want-to-achieve-them

<u>Bonus Content</u>

As a bit of a bonus, I want to add value to you for purchasing the paperback version of this book.

I believe that all of the content shared with you so far has given you the tools necessary to make some powerful changes in your mindset, as well as how you prepare for future opportunities to grow yourself. Now, when you take on a new role or position, change jobs, tackle a stretch goal or just wake up for a new day, you will have the ability to identify aspects of your mindset that are going to try to drag you down. You will also be able to more easily identify the positive aspects of your mindset that can help build you up and give you strength in the challenging times.

It all starts with the ability to **Recognize** (as you likely recall as the first of the 3Rs), then you can take action from that point to **Replace** and **Reshape** your mind so you can be a powerhouse on the battlefield…or wherever you are or whatever you're doing. You have the ability to be amazing at it! Remember, you can and will do this!

Okay, so that rah-rah session is over. I just wanted you to know that _you are powerful when you put an equipped mind to work_.

Now, I want to share with you something that I know will help you become even more powerful and effective.

The **Power of Focus** is an important and essential part of the holistic mindset health. Numerous people have used a popular phrase, "What you focus on expands." Whether in personal or professional aspects, it is true either way.

If we focus on the positive, we attract the positive, and vice versa. If you are anything like me, and some others that I know, what happens when you drive down the street, see a pothole and look at the pothole, all the while thinking, "I sure hope I miss that pothole!?!" Pothole wins! However, if in the same scenario, you see the pothole, determine to miss the pothole and look off to the side to navigate the path to clear it, you *typically* clear it.

There are actually two lessons in this example:
1) you have to first **recognize** the pothole…reference back to Step 1 in this Mindset Inventory Exercise™.

2) when you focus on where you want/need to go, instead of where you don't want/need to go, you have a much greater chance of success.

Now, some potholes (read: any situation in life) that are huge and harder to navigate. However, if you happen to miss the mark, or perhaps you didn't identify a hazard soon enough, that gives you a chance to learn for the next time something challenges you.

So, if you notice, my *focus* there was on the positive aspect of the outcome, not the fact that you hit the pothole, or the challenge got the best of you. It is all in the perspective that you develop as part of your natural state of mind…your mindset.

I have often been asked, "How can you find the positive in just about any situation?" Well, the answer is simple, that is my natural state of mind…how I am wired at this point in my life. That does not mean that I am so naïve to think that there is nothing negative out there. Quite the opposite actually. I see lots of negative all around me, I just chose not to let that be my point of focus. I **recognize** and keep my focus on what is important to me in that situation. I embrace the **Power of Focus**, realizing that "What I focus on expands."

As I close out this bonus section, I want to leave a couple questions, a challenge and a quote. I will start with the quote.

Larry Kendall, author of Ninja Selling, is one of the people with believes in the **Power of Focus.** He states in his book, *"Focus on what you want…What you focus on expands."*

My **questions** for you are:

1) What do you want…out of life, relationships, work, business, recreation, finances, etc.?
2) What focused actions will you take to achieve that which you want? Perhaps even rank them.

The **challenge** is this: Answer those questions completely, then, on a separate paper/document, <u>write everything out so you can review it.</u> Annotate <u>what you want</u> in any/all of the areas you chose, and <u>the focused actions</u> you are going to take to create the results you want to see.

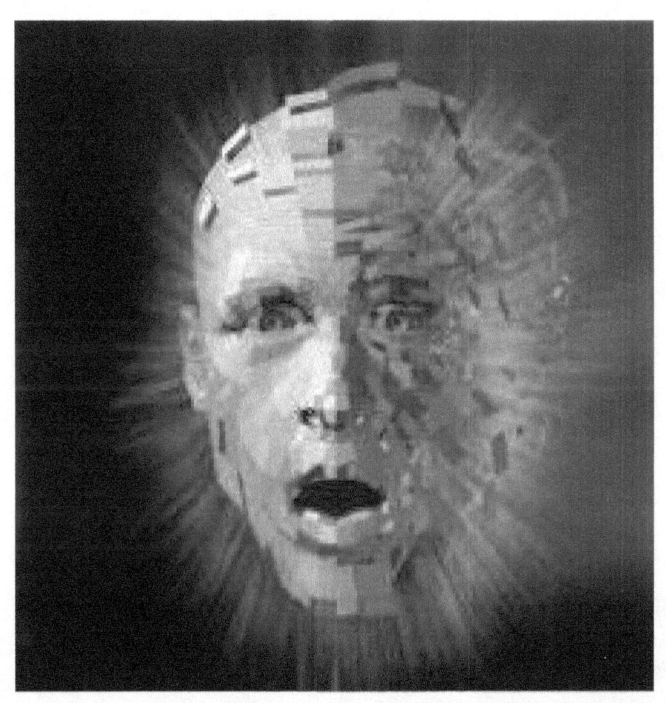

HIGHER CALLING CONSULTING, LLC

Enjoy the new arrows you have in your quiver.

You can complete this exercise any time and as many times as you see fit.

Please reach out to me with any questions.

You Have
Saved Time & Saved Money

HIGHER CALLING CONSULTING, LLC

Leadership expert with nearly 30 years of military leadership experience. I develop Entrepreneurs, Leaders and Executives so they can show up at their very best for themselves and their teams.